Getting

Written by Tracey Michele

Picture Dictionary

bus

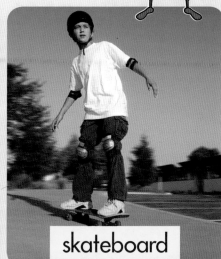
skateboard

sailboard

sled

There are many ways for people to get around.

Some people walk to get around.
They walk to school.
They walk to work.
Some walk fast.
Some walk slow.
They get the energy they need
from food.

sidewalk

These people are walking around the city.

Some people
take a bus to get around.
The bus gets the energy it needs
from fuel.
Fuel makes the bus go.

This man is taking a bus to work.

wheelchair

Some people ride a bike
to get around.
They push the pedals
with their feet
to make the bike go.
The pedals move the chain.
The chain turns the wheels.

What Makes a Bike Go?

chain

pedal

Some people cannot walk around.
They cannot take a bus.
They cannot ride a bike.
They use a sled to get around.
Dogs pull the sled
to make it go.

huskies

A team of huskies
is pulling the sled.

Some people cannot take a bus.
They cannot ride a bike.
They use a sailboard
to get around.
They use the wind
to make their sailboard go.

This man is sailing his board on a lake.

wet suit

Some people get around
on a skateboard.
They push with their foot
to make the skateboard go.
The skateboard takes them along.

helmet

This boy is skateboarding around town.

Activity Page

1. Think about ways your friends get to school.

2. Draw a school bus with all your friends on it.

3. Write two sentences about what makes the bus go.

Do you know the dictionary words?